Ilma Rakusa

Love After Love

Translated from German by Paul-Henri Campbell

SurVision Books

First published in 2021 by
SurVision Books
Dublin, Ireland
Reggio di Calabria, Italy
www.survisionmagazine.com/books.htm

Original German edition, entitled "Love after love", was published by *edition suhrkamp 2251*
© Suhrkamp Verlag, Frankfurt am Main, 2001

Copyright © Ilma Rakusa, 2021

Translations © Paul-Henri Campbell, 2021

Cover image © Annelies Štrba, 2021

Design © SurVision Books, 2021

ISBN: 978-1-912963-03-4

This book is in copyright. No part of this publication may be reproduced, stored in a retrieval system or transmitted in any form or by any means without the prior permission in writing from the publisher.

Acknowledgements

Four nine-line poems from *A Farewell to Everything* (Shearsman Books, Exeter, 2005; transl. by Andrew Shields and Andrew Winnard) reprinted in the *Afterword* by kind permission of the original publisher.

CONTENTS

Nevermore	5
Everywhere	14
Nowhere	23
Limbo (I)	28
Limbo (II)	31
Limbo (III)	35
Lament	39
And Venice	45
Love's Whispered Inventory. *Afterword by Paul-Henri Campbell*	49

Love After Love contains eight long-poems that focus on an *amour fou*, a passionate amorous obsession and a tragedy that lasted five years in the life of the author, when she fell in love with a jeweler. This book is about love after its innocence has been lost. Ilma Rakusa's poetry leaps from fondness to bitterness, from lust to disgust, from anger to sorrow in heartbeat. Often the language arrives at a sort of litany, a Kaddish, and culminates in a manic, swirling tone. The original German has an embedded dialogue with an Englishman. We have decided to offer these "English originals" *in italics*, while the translation is in regular type. The reader will find in these poems an author who is careening onwards through a flurry of emotions. These poems chronicle a long-distance relationship gone awry. They also record an asymmetric relationship, and in doing so poetically adjudicate acts of cruelty between a man and a woman: gaslighting, as well as domestic violence. But despite this, these poems are preeminently a touching testament to the contradictions of love, the stubbornness of lust, and the desire to love, to devote, to resign oneself to another heart. From its retrospective vantage point, *Love After Love* is ultimately an attempt at regaining selfhood and a catalyst for the soul.

Nevermore

Scaredy-cat is chasing me now, lily-livered, whisking me away.
Now or never, wrath. Like wound like Voodoo.
No "likes", please. *No similes, please*. Just wrath. Pure wrath.
She harms herself. And had been doing so for a while.
Chipping away at her core. This strange lust.
This obedient, whorish lust. Cutting into the flesh.
Deep, deep down.
And she shouts and whores around. *Oh, it hurts so badly*.
Smack in the face. After a good beating. Hard to the heart.
Right where you twitch and twist. Right in your eye.
You! What? Can't do anything right. Forget about it.
The hammer hit the mark, though. *Wrong*.
Cold shower and oh how I love. No yes you.
Because you will stomach even more. Blows. Draining yourself. Entirely.
Get some exercise, *move your ass*. Jack yourself up for *fun*. What's
up with that Russian drama, baby?
Get out. Into life. Don't watch that ship sail away from the port.
Quick, quick and hey twitch and obey.
And sifting. Thoroughly. Wheat from the chaff. *It's so easy*.
Exchanging rings. This moment doesn't know
its own name.
Because we're rushing into it. Why? No! You're stupid.
Because. Rushed it like into meals like into cooking. Hot.
And all those tongues lungs burnt. *It's so easy*.
He is. The boss the chevalier the Grim Reaper.
Now! High on horse into battle! And the battle cry:
possession.
I want you. Like crazy. From top to ... denuded, *my
lovely lovely girl*.

As naked as the heart. That clamoring clump.
Oh God, don't pick apart that heart. Leave a hole,
a retreat, oh.
Retreat into numb pain. *Drainage*.
And what isn't enough, isn't enough. Because you're freaking leaking.
Man-of-war with a wolfish leaking soul. Whatever
is pumped into you, is flushed out to nowhere.
And also hard currents, confessions, *big passions*, ovations.
Boy, you're wrecked. It's pouring out of me, forth, why, what for?
You? Can't hold it. Plug the leak. Lousy exchange.
What is scooped out of me,
counts towards the leakage.
In and away, oh. And where there are whales, you are not.
Endless fatal demands! More, now, all of it!
(That's how Callas sold herself away and sang into the sea.)
All of it.
The great trap. The riot of impatience: *Your circle is
complete. You you you*.
I am the circle. I am the sheep. I am guilty. I am
being punished.
So easy, disaster. And roles are assigned
forever. Frustration.
While lust thrives in summer.
A kingdom. A playing field. Take it and *fuck*.
The face so trusting and open, a body of joyous flesh. All of it.
Hand on schlong.
Fumble around, space and time, gone. Two hearts happily united.
No, you I thee me, all bets are off.
Bonding fondling.
And a sleepy lovefest, the win-win of emptiness.
Gently breathing. For
now, amen.
Beyond the hedges there's stillness. Behind the curtains,

your illness. Approaching death.
I am falling.
How long do you think I'll put up with that?
So fucking destructive.
The theta of death throws its thin long line,
leading me to you.
So fucking perverted.
A thin line, my love.
I can't reach you!
Six thousand miles don't throw tantrums. Get on the phone.
And then? what?
Imagination will play its games.
That phony jellyfish.
We fuck on the phone.
Sweety, I'll lift your skirts!
Twilight descends upon the house, the furniture, the plants. Panting voices. And in the undergrowth of emotions love loves itself.
Itself.
This is where it starts to get complicated.
The enormous project increases in scale.
Blossoming, climaxing, fogging up, in a trance.
We stagger through the mist. We are floating. On the pillow.
All-or-nothing.
Oh, like being *high*. Heroic. Insanity on the brink of the abyss.
Because you don't … me, but my image. But love. But yourself.
Because the dream is shattered to pieces, confronted with reality.
No daily routines, *please*!
Phone calls, frantic and hypnotic.
Airport concourses, hotel rooms with dimmed lights.
Where there are no roots, desire latches on.
My nomadic chieftain knows this to be a fact.

Instincts are instincts.
And the force of attraction increases tenfold
when the weight of things is removed.
Light, sizzling, jolt, lightning. Corporal convulsions.
We are. All of a sudden locked in. To each other. Without return.
The reigns tight, bridled passion.
Darling, I am addicted to you.
Stupidity gallops straight into submissiveness.
And she who is submissive, must swallow it all.
I already am. Like? *Inadequate, guilty.*
A punching bag with long legs. *Nice long legs.*
Well-toned for further disqualifications.
Desire like punishment like desire like...
Double password. Unlocked. You've got me.
Under your spell.
Like birds darting off every which way out of the dark hedges.
Into the black air. Suddenly, with a stunted cry.
I'd like that too. To get out, out. If courage is lacking. To cut it off.
Fly away. Oh spellbound, oh man. *What did you do to me?*
I love you passionately.
Right.
Who'd buy that. Pain breaks passion. Doubt rattles the cages.
Reality rears its head. *Nasty little thing.*
Rebellious sons, cadaster plans. *Fuck.*
Yanked out of it. Pulled out of the arrangement. Easily said.
With a swallow's charm skyward, out of your piercing embrace.
Overpowering overwhelming. How much longer?
Am I fooling myself?
Remorse? No. *No regrets.* No, no. I met you on a plane.
I considered it to be fate. With your brown shoes, your big smile.
Fate, you know. So, don't boss me around.
But the boss is the boss. And what falls into your lap, isn't enough.
Never enough. I want it my way.

Period.
The warrior has spoken.
His gaze, steel-grey.
Then we're arguing.
And later delve into dreamy reveries.
There, a crying child. *Relentless.*
Chewing its tears in its mouth.
What wound?
Why?
You mean goodbye?
Grinding the goodbye ax.
Hardly through the door, already gone again.
Hardly given, taken. Hardly promised, retracted.
Hardly a day that says: I am. Curtailed, cut up, time.
In the four-sided span of measured encounters.
Arrival, departure. Now!
But the heart is hurrying up and thus is consumed.
In that arrangement. Vacuum.
Deprivation, calling.
The squadrons of the unlived.
Oh, add-on dream. Temptation.
Man-high deprivation.
You charmer, you imposter,
you waster of energies, you devourer of souls.
Oppressor.
All those lovely words: I'm lucky to have you.
Remember, I care.
I caress you.
The square is empty.
Nobody.
Merely the squadron is still raging.

And there was that night in Dorset.

Full of woolly sheep in the creamy fog.
The headlights unable to cut through it.
Step by step we were fumbling forth.
We wanted to visit the coast, the cliffs.
Inhale the scent of seaweed. And ended up turning around.
When the fog lifted, there was a house surrounded by oak trees.
And a bed. No storm. Moonlight.
Why depart. Into the impossible.
Your urge.
Urgent, your urgency.
Because.
Faster, fastest.
Fire aim ready
Fire!
And what was planned, was cancelled.
Do, do. *First*. Think. *Second*.
And I am catching up on a delay. *Too slow, too late, too passive, too.*
A terrified creature facing your headlights.
Or fetch me out of the corner, relocated for discipline.
You can't do it. You don't know me.
Enough. Who are you?

My sorrow is not my ecstasy.
What was killed, rises up from books, songs, garments, beds.
Where have you not been?
With your aisles, cleared paths.
You, doer. Ruler. Gobshite. Berserker.
God, I grieve.
The letters engraved. Into me. The voice.
Word for word.
To stamp you out. Is my job.
Damn surgery. Damn that midday hour.
The mild sunlight. The carefree birds.

The love in the trees.
And my face: blind.
My house: renunciation.
Get out of here!
Leave me, lover. The siege is over.
The stronghold will woo itself. Ruined. But free.
Will woo and free itself, *lover*. Joyous desperation.
Don't cry.
Don't be shy.
And the pendulum is swinging: No.
No plaything no more. For your impatience.
For your desire and destruction.
I am. I, myself.
For the rest of my life.
Cloud, butterfly.
Youthful?
You've awakened the girl, taken her to the dance. She lives on.
Despite of you.
But o, renunciation.
Can't see your square feet. Your frizzy ear. Looking for you.
The despicable paradox: *I miss the bliss. But it can't be you.*
Kisses out of the blue.
Traitor.
Of artificial paradises.
An enormous swindle, all of this.
And wiggle and squirm until I am sore.
How could this be possible? How could I allow it?
Out of fascination construction.
Out of construction obstruction.
The autopsy followed soon thereafter.
Of a living
body. You ravager of corpses.
You are killing me! I shouted

up to the innocent ceiling of the hotel room
and ran ran and through Central Park. Away and beyond.
You remained loudly absent.
Like someone who knows the law to be on his side.
Mister Number Cruncher: checked your gains, losses.
Covered bills or not.
Percentage, price, cost, etcetera.
Oh, how appropriate. To extend your business into your love life.
Thee me I you. And the balance sheet.
And: the judge.
Because Mister Lawful dishes out penalties.
Teasingly: *learn to deal with consequences!*
A rumbling afterthought: *now!*
I am already running running.
Into the harbors of fear,
home into my childhood kingdom
to be safe.
Leaving nothing but blows and garter tights.
The stick and the carrot.
The black combo.
And when you see me crouching
just tap your self-aggrandizing hat.

More, more, everything!
From which follows: *nothing.*
And we drank the magic potion, the shrewd water,
waves of rapture, woe, warmth
wondrous words, celestial offerings
wild pleasures
sleep
sleep
in your hollow hand
so homely

(and connubial)
with white moth orchids
resolute while waiting
exuberant reunions
you tossed me up in the air
airport air *my lovely lovely girl*
you dominator of my heart
we hung suspended on the hooks of desire
and during voyages
we were the swift wheels
rolling towards our destination:
the game of lust.
My boy, my dear devil
your shaft's stiff bliss
in my lap
and more and more
and do it again
and again

Wow.
The dream is over.
The days shrouded in shadows. All of them grey and alike.
Nevermore.
Do you realize?
Time whisked away, autumn descending
upon the land. Leaves falling,
falling as though from afar.
We've been sundered.
And what is now.
And what is.
And what.
And.

Everywhere

How does one give up, when one loves.
Just leave, over, and no longer continue
love that is constant. Certain places,
to leave them, a room, a street, everything
that once affected you.

—Endre Kukorelly

There you are
on the meadow among swaths of hay
on Lüder Glade
in the chestnut grove
on Maira Bridge
on the Roman road
in the kitchen empire
you are on the serpentines
on the sofa, at the trout pond
on paths, in the garden
in front of the bending apsis
on the graveyard gravel of San Martino
at the village well, at Negozio
like a bung
on my tongue
in my lung
is there any place where you are not
beneath an apple tree
on the dancefloor
at the market in SoHo
on Fifth Avenue down at Mesa Grill

bidding farewell at the gates of the Royalton
you are on the steps leading up to the foyer
at Gotham's, in the Village-Café
in the shower temple (I am waiting
in my negligée)
on the squares with pigeon ads
in the subway tunnel
watching the ice-skaters in Central Park
hand in hand with me or no
so very apart
you are everywhere
my fucking sweetheart
Sting, singing your melody in the cab
the lagoon welcomes you knee-deep with your face
Giardini Riva the Campo Fantin
you are the hare and the tortoise and
my phobia
off to the Venetian lions, to Harry's Bar, to the Deux Magots?
your brown jacket rushes ahead
opens the door for me
the books are peering at me, the bed
the coffee, with your inquisitive gaze,
more alien than ever
am I? and sorry where am I?
alone, divorced
in limbo
between here and there
between then and now
in the dominium of stray dogs and revenants
knocked out

aren't you waving right there on the corner
are you hiding behind the tree?

am I not seeing your eyes
filled with virginal joy?
off to the forest for a rose-fingered sunset
off to the Blue Duck for dinner
off to the Golden Ram
out late for a bit of Jazz
move your ass, darling
love, homemade
a stroll in the old town
the moon has risen high
the swans are sleeping in
the shadow of the boat
and we, lovers,
a couple

therefore: done and over
a key
flung into the night
the hotel room white
and empty
you're gone
and the little room is in mourning
my house has been abandoned
even the dog senses
he won't return
he
devastating, the power of
deficits
something is screaming and screaming
the shoes the table
the stone in the window
the walls
and I

defunct
defused

why do you hate me
yourself?
from the city's canyons
the clamor
and high up into the face
hot the weight
of your hand
warning: speak
the truth
how does one count the sand?
you're kidding yourself, idiot
what is true is: we are
children of the wind
you
a warrior
and I
a fool of desire
hooked on you
and our reveries
on all four legs
do I look for you
up and down the country
with sandals wings
you'll arrive on *flight no. 1*
when the morning dawns
when the heart's ice thaws
and

flowers
welcome home

a hullo a kiss
a long slumber
don't let me go
no never
and don't punish me
with your oceans
stay
shed off the miles
stay
take me now
and hold me in your arms
give me warmth
Europe is sleeping
I am your house your continent
I love you
the rain is silent
fall asleep

while sleeping
the guns are put aside
only long ago in Dorset
the flies
filling the room with noise
we lay
outside, sheep
the spray kills whatever it can kill
we smell
foreign
a narrow bed
you are drawn in by the night
that's where we lost each other
lies? you say
I imagined the walls as you did

the door the pool
the sparsely furnished
living room
the tiled bathroom
the square yard
the white roof
the clean-cut proportions
of the windows the limestone
the sloping driveway
beneath the hill
the grand piano and space
for books
the sofa (*oversized*) the chairs
the long table
you and me at the fireside
snuggled up
the mistral wind beating outside
or a sad struggle
sometimes
huddling in silence
I pictured us both
saw the movie in my head
but how do
pictures become a home?
so much terrain and undergrowth
and thorns thistles grass
gorse holm oak thyme
lavender so much boxwood and
mistletoe and stalks
so much of everything
the end

you're crying? the wilderness is
sprawling out unimpeded
doesn't want a purchasing agreement
I stumble over the blades of grass
don't hold me
tight
build your nest
when the time will come
let's keep the shared memories
oh Man of Sorrows
and forget

the rupture
tearing into the heart
winter is long
winter is snow
Provençal slopes blown over
flurries
and Venice seems further away
than ever, never before
kiss me, lover
where will we be one
in which scenery
will we be
whole

or without drama
a vicious circle
don't shout
the woods are watching
with its creatures
father will hear it in his grave
don't put me on death row

don't condemn me
don't stab at the wound

another round
and warm
and water
and thermal springs in the mountain
with a black sound chamber
your OM is resounding in the heavens
seeping deep into the clouds
like relief
you are hovering like a star
beneath the domed ceiling
this is how still it is within us
we turn
home to the mothers
you're tired now
and I am tired
timelessness
primordial time is weird
and free

of anger
a strand of hair black
indifferent
you murmur, *no agenda*
calmly
so calm before the storm
I don't see it coming
not in the bathroom
not in front of the bell tower
in Ilanz
not during the drowsy excursion

through town
where everything came full circle

at the hotel

we couldn't do it at that time
I left you alone
now the river is fading in the dawn below the window
I am with you
disheartened
you cheer me up
caressing your bride
almost in passing
out of habit
like a friend and comrade

but it was the last time

hard to believe
so very hard
what shall I do with the streets
squares
nets for our seeds?
do you hear me?

Nowhere

> *We are; but it's nowhere.*
> *Somewhere is nowhere?*
> *Somewhere is anywhere.*
> *Is anywhere everywhere?*
> *Is anywhere somewhere?*
> *Everywhere's nowhere?*
> *everywhere?*
> *everywhere*
> *everywhere?*
> *everywhere*
> *nowhere?*
> *nowhere*
> *no*
> *where?*
>
> —Robert Lax

Haven't roped in anything in a while
I flung the lasso out to Britain (*one hour less*)
to New York (*six hours less*), to L.A. (*nine hours less*)
a rope cast across oceans time zones lifestyles
nothing is in sync, everything is disjoint
you're there, I'm here
you're with dolphins, I'm in the belly of
the night
don't laugh
today the Japanese bush is glowing
and the homeless
will winter where

the depreciated District of You and Me
with coffers clothes blazing ire
I'm cold you're cold or not
in the sky
within the creatures with engines and propellers
there is your place,
flying from here to there,
away
and utterly without return
in Nowhereland
where, long ago, our paths crossed
your hand took my hand
don't be afraid
and my coyness vanished
the storm passed by
during Disney at breakfast, European sunshine
we exchanged contacts (come visit me!)
F-16 bombers over Sarajevo
but far
but you are as jolly as a child
childish over and over
and later on, your imperious demands
impatient: *all at once*
with a demeanor saying: me me me
and me again
and that Me is inflated like a balloon
too inflated to stay and stay a while
taking space
a lump
we can't do it
you shout
I cry
you are strong like a bull

demanding more and more
I beg you: consume less
you go nuts
I am barely more
than a blade of grass
thin and green
a paraphrase
of myself
you are a man
of action pimp and tormentor
I am a woman
mouse-grey at times
and not considered smart at all
I am your acre
and whatever your dick
accomplishes –
is turned to dust
by our discrepancy
so
so each time
in a three-week rhythm
in a turbulent pact
a real test of talents
phobia ridden
better leave
easier said than
where fantasy
ponders harmonies
and the self
is suspended on a tightrope
held by the other person
the giver of life
defiler of life!

between betrayal
and portrayal
a phoneline
a singular string,
a hairline marking
the difference between
step and misstep
dynamite –
and cut
and galloping into the off
oh treasured scene
and the urge to go back
into the bliss of force
once
twice
again
slave away each time
poke around in the pain
aching for that heart thrill
do you love me?
or not?
what do you feel?
what do you think?
we are battling for whatever
is escaping us
gradually tightening the noose
tighter
laboring for calamity
listen:
it can't go on
time's up
the wrath has waned
desire is defeated

and love eloped
somewhere, far away
but not anywhere close to us
within these suffering partners
within their fearful quarters
but not within us
in our craving
woe
so cold
this world
the hedges
where red was, snow is
greeting
where green was, ice is
the birds are taking flight
the lake is frozen stiff
and the house
in paralysis
I know you know
it's over
or not
have some tea
four o'clock
everything else –
is fate

Limbo (I)

1. region on the border of Hell
2. Hell, Hades
3. prison, durance
4. border, edge
5. zombie-like condition

Falling for
and down below the ground breaks away
totally gone
apropos, below: where
the damned band of birds is peeping
in heart tones
late fall
the yellow fallow leaves the clean sweep
of late hope
to be happy takes quite
a lot
the children are playing
no longer in the field
only dogs are making
their hurried rounds
and
chestnut smoke
the venison is served freshly
(game food festival) a feast
the cooks have long ears
afterwards on thin shoe soles
back home
in the rain

who's calling?
the silhouette of Syria
fixated in my head
with deserts rivers
bare bleak mountains
from above
everywhere fallow land
apropos, above: ether blue
knows no climate zones
and where I am
doesn't matter a bit
a dreamy flight
that never again hit the runway

a hovering plea
take your feet down
walk through the mud
through November depths
it sounds like
chirping
(the conscience bugged by whimsies)
while wrinkles
fall
from the fraying
face
and

across the sky no ocean
in sight, vertically,
dizziness stings
Vertigo
honey-yellow is God
(*reluctant gravities*)

I go out and
come in
and can't find
that place

the star like a barn floor
like a carpet like a dovecot
nothing but leaves in the garden
heaps of leaves
and a chair
snoozing
so that's that
one or two blissful tricks
and downfall
so indifferent, so unpleasurably
flesh

egress to ingress

is love lightening up
in limbo, Mr. Edge?

Limbo (II)

Red of the bells on wool mittens
red of the rowanberry on a devastated mouth
red of the flames in the hearth
redbreast red or carmine red
red of the carpet from Bukhara
call red and everything's sore
I mean: who around here is totally ablaze?
we are just smoldering
between bed fear and
nowhere

choking
the room beaten down
the only light
from above out of a cannula

may I might I
move
a long wait
as heaven is as windy as the Holy Night
stale, my appetite
seduced by power
when words are blown to smithereens
thus I lay awake
shaken, I try to take shelter
but
no arm shields me
no foothold, no sheets
simply

I myself
and the redbreast is on my mind,
singing its colder melodies

snow head
flurries migranoid
with Venus moon, Swiss pine, ancient laments
with goldfinch, teardrops, expired dreams
with tassels, hooves, hullo-shouts
and pain

in those days the child is
alone with the sea
in the auburn house
was that me?
the sky lost in currents
and even more alone than ever
a steep coastline forehead *chambers in the heart*
the one for you, the rest put aside
wounded

red isn't a great color for weddings
now you are hellish dead
and the sea over there
a parting sea, separating us

hooting itself into a fit

I've already forgotten
why the day gets out of bed
nothing ever lasts
as poppy-seeds fall
morals drop

and our moon
smashed in Hades

kiddo, was that misery
nimble and shifty
how meager our claims
consumed in the gap of promise

exult once
high hypnosis
with swaying stairways
up in the sky
but it is not to be
wet shock
downwards in a fury
into the vault of all lore
into the netherworld
down where chimeras roar

an empty firmament
and gutted rooms
but memories scream upon my cheeks

the first Paris trip the first annoyance
the dance and the iron on the dancefloor
scratches
a ruined rendezvous
punched out complaints
children's mittens (my substitute for animal fur)
your back fleeing me
the cuts and cries
no farewell kiss
but waiting is always madness

down on all fours
doggish

the afternoon is rowing away
the evening the night
the following day
(where am I)
a prisoner of memory
don't make me
chew on bare bones

worried boundary or bone

in the treetops the redbreast
is breeding us

too late

out of two nests no fledging egg

only smashed

Limbo (III)

disenfranchised
dispirited
disfigured
disgraced
disrespected
discouraged
disheveled
despised
dismembered
disjointed
dispossessed
disembodied
desecrated
dishonored
distressed
deserted
discarded
discredited
disdained
disconcerted
disparaged
disheartened
disloved

That's it, I say.
My sky fell on the street.
And silence.
Where do words fall in place
if head and heart are split apart

I mean nowhere
and on the streets of London
another woman strolls by your side

Stop!
the call brushes your collar
falls
you say: done
without even turning around
that's supposedly my life
the gap between knowing and pain
meadow of madness
an enormous knife
cutting, tearing

please, not like this
alone
in a tent of blankets
at pillow-morning
dead nights
or who is pushing whom off the stage

a film gone white
dreams bleached

where is the dream? I'm waiting
our lungs doing teamwork
our tongues
done?

a nightmare
weighing twenty stone
you're on top

I'm without skin

you fuck
you leave
you've left

*I am caught
in one body*

cramp splinter raw dark

language fails

swords

now that belittled being is rummaging
in her own littleness
taunts the heavens
hand between legs
all the time
tongue touching teeth
mine
mine
carrying blood
locked in there
because you've locked me out
out in
bewitched by
bring me back home
no
leave me be
no
liver spleen quarrelling

brain pineal gland
desire comes legs apart
lays there red
renews itself
wants you

you declare yourself dead

the bread hurts

I am a pigpen
of foul feelings

thus the flesh twists and turns
on itself
echoless
defeated by darkness
counting the seconds of agony
time, a rubber band

what's next

bed
breath
death

no

Lament

Wintertime nighs;
But my bereavement-pain
It cannot bring again;
Twice no one dies.

—Thomas Hardy

I will unfurl you
along your places
you, the unpossessable
I will release you
into the rolling hills
into the pebbled beach
Chesil Beach
Weymouth
Wyke Regis
Chickerell
Fleet
Charlestown
Overcombe
West Chaldon
Holworth
Osmington
Friar Waddon
Rodden
Godmanstone
Up Sidling
Dewlish
Hermitage
Cerne Abbas

Sandhills
Puddletown
Mappowder
Whatcombe
Durweston
Dorchester
Sherbourne
Longburton
West Knighton
Warmwell
Owermoigne
East Morden
Poxwell
Kimmeridge
Witchampton
Tumworth
Cheselbourne
Bere Regis
Woodrow
Frome St. Quentin
South Perrott
Holstock
Yetminster
Spetisbury
Wraxall
Ibberton
Plush
Broadmayne
Binnegar
Leigh
Portesham
Askerswell
Creech

Furzebrook
Cattistock
Uploders
Bincombe
Evershot
Droop
Woolland
Powerstock
and
Piddletrenthide
Minterna Magna
Sydling St. Nicholas
with its mossy
churches churchyards
with brooks geese
thatched roofs pubs
with oaks
with pheasants hares
and paths hedges
with sheep, woolly,
dappled sheep
and hills
and puddles
and

as a child already,
you wandered off
into the landscape
away from home
left
stubborn: *they don't appreciate me*
away, only to return, with a satchel etcetera
at night or at dawn

a teddy a plate was all you needed
your rations
that's your old pattern
bargaining for love

and?

time after time
you take
you leave
and almost get it
and leave
and let it go
and are spoiled
and leave
and discover novelties
in the old
and want it again
and leave
and take
and leave
and can't understand
why
because you lost sight of that
two faces on one coin
(Dr. Jekyll and Mr. Hide)
a shipwreck
and you search
and avoid
yourself
you get up
you leave the house
the wife

the blessing
in anger or
emboldened by madness
a man
a man
capable of anything
allowed to do anything
who wheels and deals
and leaves
I can't see you any more

distress blowing cold
you slowly vanish

you're gone

Once upon a time there was a mouth that said: you
once upon a time there was a hand that gently soothed
once upon a time there was an ear that never withdrew
once upon a time there was a voice that uplifted anew
once upon a time there was a suitcase that had time
once upon a time there was a coat that flew by design
once upon a time there was a dream that let us chime
once upon a time there was a song that knew ceaseless sunshine
once upon a time there was a wish that grew enormously
once upon a time there was a kiss that stung like a bumblebee
once upon a time there was a day that forever shaped my destiny

and only death to get you out

the hills hollowed out

the names empty in a row
names

my amen follows you
westward
into the twilight of reason

peace?

on the atrophy of love
even the nursery rhymes
escape you
without comfort
a titmouse
in the frost
sky
where are
you

And Venice

It's all still here
Riva San Stae
Santa Maria Formosa
the Campo San Fantin
the vegetable barges at San Barnaba
the gondola graveyard the antiquarian
the Egyptian lioness at the Arsenale
slender and skeptical as ever
the Giardini's boxwood garden
sandy paths children's swing
the pavilion
Carpaccio's "St. George and the Dragon"
"St. Ursula's Dream"
the Cimitero
the mosaic gold of the basilica
Santa Maria Assunta
the reeds and the boats
and Harry's Bar
the lagoon azure Burano
Titian's Pietà
the leaning towers and bridges
the Trattoria Colomba
it's all here
the Vaporetti Traghetti
steamboats bulwarks and bollards
the Pensione Accademia
the redbrick walls
the Palazzi Piazze
the carnival masks

Tintoretto's Scuola
Zattere and Santa Elena
marble moss stairs
algae and
Colleoni's equestrian statue
the Ghetto
San Marco's flock of doves
it's all here
only the four Tetrarchs
in red porphyry
their embrace is missing
and you
master

the sunset
is toying with the couples
light water reflection
I need a shoulder

why Venice then?

the Angel of Annunciation
beating its wings against
the door slammed shut

how much waiting can a person
bear
until nevermore

angelic salutation
or a blow of the hoof
cold ammo
waiting I am weary as a broken pillar

come
come
into the gold of byzantine icons
the aureoles
come into the heavy
rustling gardens
into the pubs
don't scream
be happy my dear rascal

plant your tree
on my stomach
while the ship's horns
are blowing outside
do it
beast

winter air
your body so calm
the act
without friction

and you and I
in collusion
like an island
snowed in
I could lift the towel from my eyes
and rise to the silence of the wooden floors

but where are you
my candle my wick?

the lions are already furious
the one named Marcus
the entire city is up and roaring
the masks the hearts
the lace-makers the forgers
black the throngs of people
even the lagoon black
the piazzas black

I stare at the ceiling
I'm guarding your snow
and melt away
waiting for the lull
that comes with night

why Venice then?
why nebule?
Bellini's angel is greeting
with the tussled fold of his gowns
and Purcell is singing:
O Solitude, my sweetest choice
falsetto *the element of noblest wit*
I know
in our messy conjunctions
there was only this: the snow and
your: I shall go

thus, the waters
will wash away
the sky

Love's Whispered Inventory
On Ilma Rakusa's *Love After Love*

By Paul-Henri Campbell

In late May 1995, Ilma Rakusa was on a return flight from Los Angeles to Zurich, having spent six weeks as a *Writer in Residence* at USC. The Swiss author looked forward to an eventless flight. Then suddenly some nearby passengers swapped seats, placing a British subject at Ilma's side. The fellow—a jeweler on a business trip to Basel—was rather chatty. As it turns out, Ilma and this unknown man relished their serendipitous tête-à-tête in the sky. After her divorce, Ilma had been living alone for several years with her teenage son on the *Zürichberg*, focused on her literary and academic work. Having loved in the past, she was no longer considering the possibility of love. But this jeweler was certainly charming. And let's be honest: what could possibly be more enticing than a flirtatious jeweler? When the plane landed in Zurich, they decided to have dinner a few days later. She agreed and invited him to her home. They read Philip Larkin's poetry and listened to Henry Purcell's *O Solitude*. In the weeks that followed, the two nascent lovers exchanged letters and soon began to talk over the phone. Two months later, they took a trip to Paris.

This short scene was the prologue to a long-distance relationship between two mature lovers who, as one might say, weren't exactly having their first rodeo. Following that weekend in Paris, they orbited around each other for five years. Passionate days or weeks together in New York, Venice, or Zurich gave way to weeks and months of longing and anticipation. Waiting for an early morning or late night phone call from the other side of the world, Ilma soon discovered that her new found lover wasn't only capable of waves of passion and endearing warmth, but also of conceited egotism and hurtful whims. So, eventually, inexorably, the relationship failed: *"Kisses, out of the blue.* / Traitor. / Of artificial paradises. / An enormous swindle, all this. / And wiggle and squirm until I am sore." (Nevermore, pg. 12).

Before I discuss *Love After Love* in the broader context of her work, I'd like to point out some peculiarities exhibited in the lines quoted above. They include features that are characteristic of the poetry in *Love After Love*. Let's first consider the opening line: *"Kisses, out of the blue"*: Any verse set in italics in my translation are already in English in Ilma's original text. The back-and-forth between German and English signifies love's dialogue. It seems as if the subject of the poem is in constant dialogue with the non-present other of the poem. A word or phrase pops up and the German poetic text is goaded on, is triggered, changes course, or responds to it. In the instance cited above, the response is rage. Now consider the second line, consisting only of a single word and a punctuation mark: "Traitor." Strangely, there is no exclamation mark after the word "traitor". Maybe the poetic voice here is pensive or containing its anger. Punctuation as well as anagrammatic line-breaks are yet another way by which the author toys with moods and attitudes. Next, the third line seems to be augmenting "traitor" by way of a genitival phrase "Of artificial paradises." But by isolating this genitive on a single line and by encapsulating it within its own punctuation, the ambience is increased, its dramatic qualities are heightened. Lastly, there is the odd line "And wiggle and squirm until I am sore," which on its face seems to be missing a pronoun "And I wiggle and squirm..." But by deleting the pronoun, the author is introducing intentional ambiguity. Who is really wiggling and squirming? By making use of poetic techniques, such as anagrammatism, truncation, or enjambement, a particular mood is established that guides the reader through this labyrinth of troubled love. Alongside such poetic devices, readers will certainly also encounter numerous literary, religious, and musical references, such as allusions to Rainer Maria Rilke's poem *Autumn*, Henry Purcell's *O Solitude*, the poems of Marina Tsvetayeva, or even the Kaddish.

The Morphology of Experience

Love After Love doesn't simply chronicle a romantic relationship, but rather accounts for and reckons with the state of mind that has been left behind. The eight long poems take their cues from those experiences and transform them into a poetic alembic, pitting voices against each other, abruptly shifting from stuttering and stammering lines to dialogue-like passages, moving from traditional rhythm and meter to colloquial verse at the drop of a hat.

The love affair so elaborately developed in *Love After Love* had already played a role in Ilma's previous poetic projects. While *Love After Love* was written in retrospect with the luxury of distance, she published a series of nine-liners in 1997 when the relationship was in full swing. That collection of nine-line poems was translated into English and published as *A Farewell to Everything* by Shearsman Books in 2005. By comparing those nine-line variations on her experiences at the time with the complex verse language of the eight long poems in *Love After Love*, the reader bears witness to the morphology of life experience throughout multiple iterations of poetic form. While the language in *Love After Love* comes from a perspective of closure, composure, and selfhood, these nine-liners reflect the throes and pain of a conflicted lover. I offer here four nine-line poems, translated by Andrew Shields (AS) and Andrew Winnard (AW) for the sake of comparison.

In tercets to you
on seahorses airplanes
frigates on angels
cupids disguised
submarines
to you on November winds
at once to escape
the sport of waiting out
the countdown

(AW)

Don't play a Russian drama you
say and your voice scratches me raw
not unscathed I fall into your
heart the child in us lame
the mouth lost
then we scuffle home to
our seas
I'll give you yours and you
me mine with esteem

(AS)

Every time the leech
of the telephone sucks away my strength
these conversations mid-air idiosyncrasies
excitement at inopportune times when there's a need
for silence or the face to go with the voice
the complete person his
weight and time to bring

the mourning slowly
under control

(AW)

You want me flat as a plane
and misjudge the mania
of such correction urbane

as you are: you refrain
from explanation on the train
of success the cellophane

world replaces the hurricane
the sorrow my bane
do you see it now? End

(AS)

But there are other contemporaneous as well as retrospective references to this love affair in Ilma's work. Having earned a PhD in Slavic philology, Ilma Rakusa published widely read essays on classics (Tolstoy, Dostoyevsky, Chekhov), on modern authors (Aleksey Remizov, Yevgeny Zamyatin, Joseph Brodsky) as well as on contemporary voices, such as Vladimir Sorokin or Valeria Narbikova. In 1995, Ilma Rakusa reviewed a novel by Valeria Narbikova. There's a strange providence in the quotes she chose from Narbikova's novel: "Why isn't it possible in life to do one thing once and for all?... Why is it impossible to be born once and for all, to fall in love once and for all, to marry once and for all? Why does it always need to happen over and over? Why does it happen all life long, the whole time?"[1] Is all literature perhaps just one enormous Rorschach test?

Having authored numerous collections of short stories, autobiography increasingly moved to the center of her work. For Ilma Rakusa, autobiography is more than recounting melancholy memories. It is a laboratory in which one might show how the mind works. Her later writing seems to be concerned with showing how selfhood emerges from a chaotic flurry of experience. At the same time, she is interested in developing poetic form that may aid, convey, and shape that realization of self to an audience as a delectable literary experience. Consider, for that matter, her memoir *Mehr Meer* (2009), based on her family story, as another example of this effort. The memoir gathers up a life story that had previously been dispersed in fragments and glimpses in her poetry and other writings. In the memoir, she describes her early childhood, having been born in Rimavská Sobota/Slovakia to a Hungarian mother and Slovenian father, and offers a fascinating story of post-war Trieste.

But in returning to *Love After Love*, I'd like to point to another utterance made by Ilma Rakusa concerning the underlying mood and deportment of *Love After Love*. It is obviously in essay form instead of verse, and was written much later:

"Poetry rarely stems from joy. It is for the most part inspired by a sense of deprivation. It has got little in common with categorical imperatives (unless it is committed to a political or religious idea). For me, writing has been an utterly incalculable event. It has transpired in the course of waiting and anxiously hoping, of listening and carefully feeling my way forward, of discarding and obeying whenever words fall into place and

---

[1] Narbikova, Valeria: Flüstergeräusch. Aus dem Russischen von Annelore Nitschke. (Frankfurt am Main;1995), cited after: Ilma Rakusa: Zauberding Rhythmus. "Flüstergeräusch" von Valeria Narbikova, in: ibid.: Von Ketzern und Klassikern. Streifzüge durch die russische Literatur. (Frankfurt am Main; 2003) Pg. 214.

come together to rhythmic clusters. An inner murmur tells me that something wants to come out onto the paper. Out of a certain mood, a sense of necessity and urgency. And if a trail comes into view that may lead forward, if lines stand firm and the rhythm pushes onward, if something suddenly holds its ground, takes a definite shape – then there is only amazement, on my part. Perhaps I might add: grateful amazement. Because success least of all follows from the mere application of tools and toys.

One may only want to speak of joy in as much as it sometimes seems unfathomable that language endures and does not fall silent. I'd never have thought that eight long poems would originate in this utter collapse of love which nearly drove me over the edge and nearly silenced me forever. They are the longest and most eccentric poetry that I ever wrote, "Love After love". Against all odds and expectations, the inner chaos took shape, gained form. And I realized that I was still alive and somewhat sane. (Later, many readers found themselves in these poems, which is another reason to speak of joy.)

The state of writing is in my case of somnambulant intensity. It is hard to grasp, and there are no witnesses, besides myself. Is it self-illuminating? Sometimes. Does it illuminate others? That is something that readers may decide for themselves. What I am absolutely confident about is that writing catalyzes. Some sort of transformation takes place on many levels. Between the real self and the subject of the poem, there are metamorphoses that are not only indebted to artistic playfulness. Whatever emerges from this, it typically has effects and repercussions. All in all, it is quite a wondrous process."

This example offers a glimpse into how life experiences morph into various literary constructs, such as the compact nine-line poem or the plethora of masks and echoes presented in *Love After Love*, or even into the elements of literary theory presented above. In her recent book, entitled *Mein Alphabet* (2019), she revisited her *amour fou*, adding it to the alphabetical index of her memories.

Loops, Lists, and Litanies

Consider the sprawling lists of place names in *Love After Love*, beginning with Weymouth and ending somewhere on a churchyard in Piddletrenthide. Ilma Rakusa's long poem *Lament* traces the voyage of two lovers in Dorset through the night. The monotony of lists is akin to the tone of the ancient eulogy, a rhetorical genre birthed by sorrow and marked by enumeration, repetition, and loops. It enacts the gyrating rhythm of sorrow, seemingly without beginning and without end. The technique has been utilized in various passages of *Love After Love*. Take note of the phonetic pleasure that comes from the endless parade of place names. In other cases, such as in the poem *Limbo (III)*, we are sucked into the vortex of a rhetorical exercise, endlessly varying verbs while keeping the verbal affix, the negative affix: "zer-"(German) or "dis-" (English). The literary strategy, built around accumulating and listing words, amasses a lexicon of disappointments, disaffection, disenchantments... and we are beyond mere wordplay but in the emotional center of gravity binding these words together. Sibylle Birrer noted in her review for the *Neue Zürcher Zeitung* that "happiness and sorrow, desire and pain spiral through the text. They spiral from the fulfilment of love towards separation. The first-person female voice is speaking to us directly bringing the elements of its lost love into order despite the chaos, thereby creating an inventory of memories."

On March 9th, 2016, Ilma Rakusa delivered the annual lecture on poetics at the *Lyrik Kabinett* in Munich. In her lecture, she returned to basics, reviewing the poetic structure of sacred music, temple hymns, the rosary, as well as the liturgical litany. "Didn't poetry originate in sacred beckoning, in summoning the powers unseen, isn't its origin prayer itself?" Her statement isn't a pious interrogative. Instead, she offers example after example of lists and loops employed by contemporary authors, such as Nora

Gomringer or Robert Lax or Thomas Kunst. This approach to theory is entirely in character for Ilma Rakusa, for her notions on poetics are not merely fancy hobbyhorses that sound great but are never really put into practice. Her literary theory is gleaned from poetry such as it is. Theory that does not work in poetic practice is not theory but fiction.

The Assertion of Selfhood

Obviously, Ilma Rakusa has been a writer for many decades. She earned her reputation by presenting short stories and literary reviews to the public across the German speaking world. In *Love After Love*, she certainly isn't interested in revising history. Despite the language of blame, of lamentation, or of sorrow, there is in this network of voices a type of subjectivity, a type of personhood that is writing from a vantage point of freedom. While one might expect the language of victimhood, the reader will find jubilant assertions of selfhood in *Love After Love*. Talking about strong women has become commonplace in these days, but discovering poetry as a type of *kintsugi* (金継ぎ), the art of the "golden repair" in Japanese ceramics, is a literary experience that not many authors can offer. Because claiming selfhood, any type of selfhood, as a poetic modus operandi is a delicate affair. Those who succeed transform the fissures, scars, and breakage into radiant patterns on objects made whole again, and those who fail in creating such poetry end up with caricatures of the Self rather than the powerful collages presented in this book.

More poetry published by SurVision Books

Noelle Kocot. *Humanity*
(New Poetics: USA)
ISBN 978-1-9995903-0-7

Ciaran O'Driscoll. *The Speaking Trees*
(New Poetics: Ireland)
ISBN 978-1-9995903-1-4

Helen Ivory. *Maps of the Abandoned City*
(New Poetics: England)
ISBN 978-1-912963-04-1

Elin O'Hara Slavick. *Cameramouth*
(New Poetics: USA)
ISBN 978-1-9995903-4-5

John W. Sexton. *Inverted Night*
(New Poetics: Ireland)
ISBN 978-1-912963-05-8

Afric McGlinchey. *Invisible Insane*
(New Poetics: Ireland)
ISBN 978-1-9995903-3-8

Anatoly Kudryavitsky. *Stowaway*
(New Poetics: Ireland)
ISBN 978-1-9995903-2-1

Tim Murphy. *The Cacti Do Not Move*
(New Poetics: Ireland)
ISBN 978-1-912963-07-2

Tony Kitt. *The Magic Phlute*
(New Poetics: Ireland)
ISBN 978-1-912963-08-9

Clayre Benzadón. *Liminal Zenith*
(New Poetics: USA)
ISBN 978-1-912963-11-9

Thomas Townsley. *Tangent of Ardency*
(New Poetics: USA)
ISBN 978-1-912963-15-7

George Kalamaras. *That Moment of Wept*
ISBN 978-1-9995903-7-6

Anton Yakovlev. *Chronos Dines Alone*
(Winner of James Tate Poetry Prize 2018)
ISBN 978-1-912963-01-0

Bob Lucky. *Conversation Starters in a Language No One Speaks*
(Winner of James Tate Poetry Prize 2018)
ISBN 978-1-912963-00-3

Christopher Prewitt. *Paradise Hammer*
(Winner of James Tate Poetry Prize 2018)
ISBN 978-1-9995903-9-0

Mikko Harvey & Jake Bauer. *Idaho Falls*
(Winner of James Tate Poetry Prize 2018)
ISBN 978-1-912963-02-7

Tony Bailie. *Mountain Under Heaven*
(Winner of James Tate Poetry Prize 2019)
ISBN 978-1-912963-09-6

Nicholas Alexander Hayes. *Amorphous Organics*
(Winner of James Tate Poetry Prize 2019)
ISBN 978-1-912963-10-2

John Bradley. *Spontaneous Mummification*
(Winner of James Tate Poetry Prize 2019)
ISBN 978-1-912963-13-3

John Thomas Allen. *Rolling in the Third Eye*
(Winner of James Tate Poetry Prize 2019)
ISBN 978-1-912963-15-7

Gary Glauber. *The Covalence of Equanimity*
(Winner of James Tate Poetry Prize 2019)
ISBN 978-1-912963-12-6

Maria Grazia Calandrone. *Fossils*
Translated from Italian
(New Poetics: Italy)
ISBN 978-1-9995903-6-9

Sergey Biryukov. *Transformations*
Translated from Russian
(New Poetics: Russia)
ISBN 978-1-9995903-5-2

Alexander Korotko. *Irrazionalismo*
Translated from Russian
(New Poetics: Ukraine)
ISBN 978-1-912963-06-5

Anton G. Leitner. *Selected Poems 1981–2015*
Translated from German
ISBN 978-1-9995903-8-3

All our books are available to order via
http://survisionmagazine.com/books.htm

www.ingramcontent.com/pod-product-compliance
Lightning Source LLC
Chambersburg PA
CBHW071757040426
42446CB00012B/2605